# THE OFFICIAL
# QUEENS PARK
# RANGERS
## ANNUAL 2020

Written by Matt Webb and Francis Atkinson
Designed by Lucy Boyd

© 2019. Published by Grange Communications Ltd., Edinburgh, under licence from Queens Park Rangers. Printed in the EU.

Photographs © Rex Features

ISBN 978-1-913034-27-6

# CONTENTS

# #WELCOMEWARBURTON

**QPR appointed Mark Warburton as the club's new manager on a two-year contract in May.**

Warburton previously managed at Brentford, Glasgow Rangers and Nottingham Forest.

Upon his appointment in W12, Warburton said: "I am delighted and privileged to be managing this club.

"When I spoke to QPR they were very clear. They have a solid plan and know what they want. They have a long term outlook and that appealed to me immediately.

"I am excited about the challenge that lies ahead."

Warburton is known for playing an attractive brand of football, and he added: "I love seeing players who enjoy their football.

"I like players being brave in possession, understanding the first thought is to play forward and be positive.

"You have to be fit as well. Work ethic, desire, hunger, passion – all those cliches are so important for us.

"Get that right, and fingers crossed we will move in the right direction."

After taking over at Brentford from Wigan Athletic-bound Uwe Rösler in 2013, Warburton steered the club to automatic promotion from League One.

In the following campaign – Warburton's only full season at Griffin Park – the newly-promoted Bees achieved a play-off place, the club's highest second-tier finish since 1934/35.

In 2015/16, Warburton won promotion to the Scottish Premiership as well as the

Scottish Challenge Cup in his first season at Rangers, while also reaching the final of the Scottish Cup.

He left Ibrox in December 2016 with them second in the Scottish Premiership. They would finish the season third.

Warburton spent nine months at Forest before leaving in December 2017.

Rangers director of football Les Ferdinand said: "This is a fantastic appointment.

"We spoke with a number of excellent candidates for the position, and Mark ticked all the boxes for us.

"He loves working with younger players and developing them, and has a great understanding of the game.

"Mark is determined to be a success and we will be giving him our full support to achieve that."

QPR chairman Amit Bhatia added: "We are all delighted to bring Mark in.

"The excellent work by John Eustace as interim manager enabled us to spend the required time speaking with suitable candidates.

"I am very pleased with how the recruitment process was carried out, as well as the end result which sees us appoint Mark as our manager."

# DID YOU KNOW?

### SEVENTIES

While he hasn't gone as far as saying he is a QPR fan, Warburton has previously stated his admiration of watching the Rangers in the mid-1970s. The ex-Brentford manager has been quoted: "That season when QPR ran Liverpool close with Givens, McClintock, Bowles, Parkes and Clement – that team had a lot of passion and I loved watching that side."

### THE CITY

Not too many clubs can say their manager used to work as a trader in the city, but that's exactly what Mark Warburton did before he became professionally involved in football. While playing in the Conference, Warburton applied for a job in a local paper that was looking for someone 'good with numbers and competitive'. That description perfectly fitted Warburton, who quit football for a life in banking and found himself working in Chicago, North Carolina and Tokyo as part of his job.

### EUROPE

After deciding to return to football, Warburton wanted to improve his knowledge of the game and learn about other styles and cultures of management. He decided to take a year out and travel around Europe to see if he could get an insight into how other clubs work. He successfully managed to spend valuable time at Sporting Lisbon, PSV, Ajax and Barcelona. Warburton's style of coaching has been heavily influenced by what he learnt on that trip.

### SQUAD

One of Mark Warburton's beliefs as a manager is that he wants to work with a small squad and use players from the academy should injuries and suspensions kick in. Explaining why he prefers this kind of approach, Warburton said: "I want players to give me everything they have in training – how can I put 19 players on a coach and say to six or seven, 'Sorry, you're not going to be involved this week'? I'd far rather go leaner than fatter in terms of squad."

### TWITTER

QPR's new gaffer is on Twitter! Warburton is an active participant on the social media platform and you can follow him by searching for **@MarkWarburton9**.

# NEW SEASON KITS REVEALED!

**QPR'S 2019/20 kits were unveiled at a special Superstore launch ahead of the new Sky Bet Championship campaign.**

The designs – first modelled by players from our First Team, Women's Team and Tiger Cubs – were created through a collaborative process between the club and our kit supplier, Erreà, in a way to innovate QPR's look and style.

It's an important return to tradition for the first shirt that revives its broad blue and white hoops.

Elegant and essential, the home shirt has a fashionable polo neck with a thin gold edging that also embellishes the sleeves.

The soft, comfortable fabric, with a double-knit construction, is characterised by the presence of tiny micro-perforations designed to ensure ventilation and optimum regulation of the body's temperature.

Breathability rounds off the characteristics of this fabric that has a 'second-skin effect' that is ideal for supporting match performances.

The same model, with clean, refined lines, is used for the away shirt which comes in a new and original aqua blue, with fine, light grey inserts.

QPR boss Mark Warburton told us: "I am really looking forward to my first season as manager here.

"There are some key moments during the close season when that first competitive game feels closer – the releasing of the fixtures and the launch of the new kits are two such examples.

"I really like the tradition and history that's associated with the QPR home strip. It is such a well-known and instantly recognisable kit and I am really looking forward to the boys running out in it."

Fabrizio Taddei, Erreà's head of pro clubs department, added: "We are very excited to be releasing our third range of QPR match kits, training and travel wear.

"While it is important for us to always maintain the hooped home tradition, we hope that everyone enjoys the new colours and designs that our designers and the club themselves have created."

Should there be a requirement for a third strip, our 2018/19 pink away kit will be utilised.

# THE SEASON THAT WAS: IN NUMBERS

**All the stats from QPR's 2018/19 Sky Bet Championship campaign...**

## 51
POINTS WON

## WINS 14
## DRAWS 9
## LOSSES 23

## 14
CLEAN
SHEETS

## 53
GOALS
SCORED

## 6 MOST ASSISTS
(FREEMAN, WELLS)

## 71
GOALS
CONCEDED

## 46%
AVG. POSSESSION

## 336 MOST AERIAL
DULES WON (SMITH)

## 1,208 MOST SUCCESSFUL
PASSES (LUONGO)

**43** MOST APPEARANCES
(FREEMAN, LEISTNER)

**7** TOP GOALSCORER
(FREEMAN, HEMED, WELLS)

**69** MOST SUCCESSFUL
DRIBBLES (FREEMAN)

**126** MOST TACKLES WON
(LUONGO)

**93** YELLOW
CARDS

**1**
RED CARD

# LUKE AMOS

HE'S ONE OF OUR OWN

# GERRY FRANCIS

# Loft legends who've come through the ranks in W12...

CAPTAIN of both club and country, Gerry Francis is undoubtedly one of the most gifted players to have ever pulled on the blue and white hoops of Queens Park Rangers.

The attacking midfielder captained England and won 12 Three Lions caps as a Rangers man.

Gerry was born in nearby Chiswick on 6th December 1951 and came up through the youth ranks in W12, making his debut as a substitute versus Liverpool on 29th March 1969.

He made 352 appearances for the R's in two spells and scored 65 times, including the BBC goal of the season in 1975/76 (also against Liverpool). He is 16th on our all-time list of Hoops appearance holders.

Francis later managed Rangers twice, masterminding a top-five finish in the first season of the Premier League in 1992/93.

"They were definitely special times in my career," said Gerry – skipper of our great team in the mid-1970s.

## "They were definitely special times in my career"

"I spent 20-odd years in total at QPR. Not too many people do that with one club, do they?

"When I played for QPR, we were runners-up by a point in the old First Division, semi-finalists in the League Cup and quarter-finalists in the UEFA Cup. I was also made England captain.

"Then when I was manager, we finished top London club in the first season of the Premier League. There's been a lot of history for me at Rangers over the years."

# NEW KIDS ON THE BLOCK

It's fair to say that the summer of 2019 was rather busy for QPR! Here's a look at a truly breathless few months in W12…

Mark Warburton was named the new QPR manager in May.

Four days later, former Brentford centre-half Yoann Barbet became summer signing number three.

The next day, defensive ace Dominic Ball was brought in after leaving Rotherham United.

Former Glasgow Rangers left-back Lee Wallace joined his former boss in W12 in mid-June.

The transfer activity continued with the loan capture of midfielder Luke Amos from Spurs at the start of July.

Former Liverpool defender Conor Masterson soon joined too on a two-year contract.

Fellow Scot Liam Kelly was also signed on June 14th – the goalkeeper joining from Livingston.

Another loanee, Matt Smith, also signed on the first of the month, from Manchester City.

The R's then contested a behind-closed-doors friendly versus Gillingham at Harlington.

Before heading out to Austria for a week of pre-season training.

QPR put on a much better display to dispatch of Oxford United on the road, in front of 1,000+ R's fans.

We were edged out narrowly against Watford in W12 in our final pre-season friendly – and introduced signings 12 and 13 (Todd Kane and Marc Pugh) at half-time.

But not before Angel Rangel re-joined on a year-long deal!

Goalkeeper Dillon Barnes swapped Colchester United for the Hoops.

Signing number 14 arrived the next day – Jordan Hugill joining on a season-long loan from West Ham.

Despite a positive first-half showing, QPR fell to defeat at Europa League outfit Austria Vienna.

Before Jan Mlakar arrived from Brighton & Hove Albion on a season-long loan deal.

Rangers got their 2019/20 Sky Bet Championship season off to a flyer, seeing off Stoke City 2-1 at the bet365 Stadium! Ebere Eze netted a goal-of-the-season contender in the win.

Rangers were then narrowly beaten at National League outfit Boreham Wood.

Summer signing number 11 (eleven) followed. Welcome back, Geoff Cameron!

Nahki Wells became our final summer signing on transfer deadline day, again arriving on a season-long loan from Burnley. Phew!

# YOU ARE THE REF

**1** A striker is impeded just outside the penalty area and you signal for an indirect free-kick. The player jumps up and quickly takes the free-kick by knocking it against the defender who had fouled him, who is still lying on the floor. The striker then shoots and the ball flies into the back of the net. What do you give?

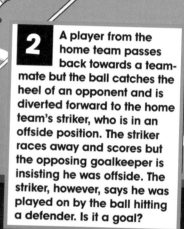

**2** A player from the home team passes back towards a team-mate but the ball catches the heel of an opponent and is diverted forward to the home team's striker, who is in an offside position. The striker races away and scores but the opposing goalkeeper is insisting he was offside. The striker, however, says he was played on by the ball hitting a defender. Is it a goal?

**3** You have awarded a drop ball inside the penalty area. One of the players who contests the drop is the defending goalkeeper who, as soon as it lands, dives onto the ball and smothers it. Is this allowed?

**4** Two opposing players jump to head a high ball and as they land one of them falls to the ground clutching his face. You call on the physio. While you are waiting you notice the big screen showing a replay of the incident, the player being treated has been deliberately and viciously elbowed by the opponent. The crowd are going mad. What action do you take?

**5** In stoppage time you award a direct free-kick to the home side. The away team, clinging to a 1-0 lead, decide to bring on a sub, then you signal for the kick to be taken. The ball flies into the back of the net but you immediately spot that the subbed player hadn't quite left the field of play. What do you do?

**6** A midfielder commits a foul worthy of a second yellow card, but you play on as the opposing team are in on goal. However, when their shot is cleared upfield it drops to the midfielder you planned to book. He collects the ball and hits a rocket which flies into the goal at the other end. What do you do?

# ANSWERS

**1 FREE-KICK** Allow the goal. Make sure you are satisfied that the player lying on the floor isn't injured AND that the striker taking the free-kick has positioned the ball correctly and then play on. You shouldn't penalise the attacking team by stopping them taking the free-kick quickly. The goal stands.

**2 OFFSIDE?** No, it is not a goal. The home player was in an offside position and has an unfair advantage so must be penalised. The law states that he is offside the moment the ball touches or is played by one of his team. The 'played onside' rule hasn't existed since 1978.

**3 DROP BALL** Yes, the goalkeeper can do this but if you deem it dangerous play for the goalie or opponent then you can give an indirect free-kick against the 'keeper.

**4 COLLIDE** You do nothing. You cannot use the big screen to help you make decisions. You should ask your assistants if they saw anything and if they didn't you then have to end the matter there. Obviously the FA can look at the incident afterwards and punish the offending player if they decide that the match officials didn't witness the elbowing.

**5 STOPPAGE TIME** The goal cannot stand and you have to award a retaken free-kick. You must apologise also for poor refereeing as play should not have been restarted until the player was totally off the pitch. Also caution the subbed player for deliberate time wasting and trying to delay the free-kick.

**6 ADVANTAGE?** No goal! It has to be disallowed and you have to show the player a second yellow and then the red. He shouldn't have been on the pitch anyway and so cannot be allowed to gain an advantage for his team. Restart with an indirect free-kick to the opposition where the original foul took place.

# FOCUS ON
# ILIAS
# CHAIR

**Nationality:**
Morocco

**Position:**
Attacking midfield

**Married:**
No

**Children:**
No

**Car:**
Mercedes

**Favourite TV Programme:**
Money Heist

**Favourite Player:**
Messi

**Most Promising Teammate:**
Ebere Eze

**Favourite Other Team:**
Barcelona

**Childhood Footballing Hero:**
Zinedine Zidane

**Favourite Other Sport:**
Basketball

**Most Difficult Opponent So Far:**
Tiémoué Bakayoko

**Most Memorable Match:**
QPR debut v Northampton

**Biggest Disappointment:**
None so far!

**Favourite Meal:**
Anything from Grandma's Kitchen!

**Misc. Like:**
I love watching American football

**Favourite Holiday Destination:**
Morocco

**Favourite Personality:**
Floyd Mayweather

**Favourite Activity On Day Off:**
Sleep!

**Favourite Musician / Band:**
Drake

**Post-Match Routine:**
Chilling with the family

**Best Friend:**
My mate Mo!

**Biggest Career Influence:**
Dad

**Personal Ambition:**
To play in the Champions League

**If You Weren't A Footballer, What Would You Be:**
Don't know!

**Person In World You'd Most Like To Meet:**
Mayweather!

# HOW TO...

# TACKLING

**Tackling is an art in football – with plenty worth considering when attempting to win the ball back from an opponent. R's left-back Ryan Manning shares his five top tips when going in for a tackle…**

## 1. TIMING

Timing is everything – especially if you plan on executing a slide tackle. A mistimed tackle could see you penalised, a player hurt or your opponents advancing into a position where they can score a goal.

## 2. STAY ON YOUR FEET?

Tackling doesn't always mean you have to slide to the ground. Sometimes it's best to stay on your feet and win possession back that way. Be clever and if you have strength, use it.

## 3. POSITION

What type of tackle you opt to make really does depend on where you are on the pitch. It's obviously never wise to dive in around the penalty area – and less of a risk away from the 18-yard box.

## 4. IS TACKLING ESSENTIAL?

Are there teammates around you? Going in for a tackle may not necessarily be the only option. If you have several teammates around you, you maybe able to win the ball back by crowding out the opposition.

## 5. COMMIT

When you decide to tackle, don't hesitate. Your opponent might then get a touch that knocks it away from you, and if you subsequently try to tackle, that may land you in hot water!

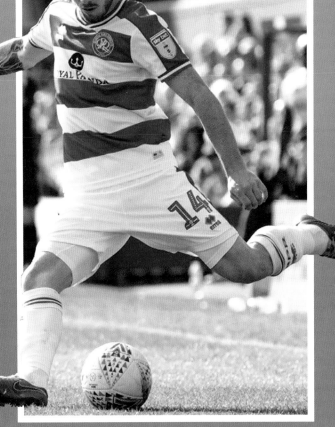

# BEST HOME WIN
## THRILLER VERSUS VILLA!

**QPR'S 1-0 victory over Aston Villa in W12 last October was probably our best home win of the 2018/19 campaign.**

Paweł Wszołek's first-half strike proved decisive for rampant Rangers, who rose to seventh in the Sky Bet Championship table with a third win in just six days.

Also collecting a seventh clean sheet in a run of 11 fixtures, this was arguably QPR's finest defensive performance yet in 2018/19, following lengthy spells of Aston Villa pressure.

It was an all-round outstanding team display from the in-form R's, who booked their fourth victory in five when Wzsołek slammed home via the underside of the crossbar in the 38th minute.

MAN OF THE MATCH

24

# THIS IS OUR CAVE

## QUEENS Park Rangers moved into our famous home ground over a century ago now.

But how has the stadium change since 1917, and what have been the standout R's moments that the stadium has witnessed? Here's a pictorial look at life in W12 through the ages...

Gerry Francis slams his first penalty for Rangers.

**NEWCASTLE PANDEMONIUM!**
Mass confusion in the Newcastle goal-mouth as Gary Bannister grabs the ball, Simon Stainrod celebrates and Glenn Roeder tries to sort out the Newcastle defence. (Photo: Martin Dalton)

**VITAL GOALS IN THE SIXTH ROUND**

CLIVE ALLEN, third from left, shoots the goal that made the result QPR 1, Crystal Palace 0 ... and took Rangers

# CHAMP CHANGES!

**AS USUAL, six fresh faces have joined us for the 2019/20 Sky Bet Championship campaign. Detailed are those new runners and riders we'll face during the season...**

## FROM THE TOP

### CARDIFF CITY

| | |
|---|---|
| **MANAGER** | Neil Warnock |
| **NICKNAME** | The Bluebirds |
| **GROUND** | Cardiff City Stadium |
| **CAPACITY** | 33,280 |
| **DISTANCE FROM W12** | 148.2 miles (2 hrs 46 mins) |
| **2018/19 POSITION** | 18th (Premier League) |

DESPITE operating on a limited budget in Premier League terms, former R's boss Neil Warnock so nearly pulled off what many deemed unthinkable in keeping Cardiff City in the Premier League.

The Bluebirds were just pipped to the final survival spot by Brighton & Hove Albion last term, but you wouldn't bet against another Cardiff promotion assault this time around.

Warnock has a record eight English promotions on his CV and will be desperate to add a ninth to catapult City straight back to the big time.

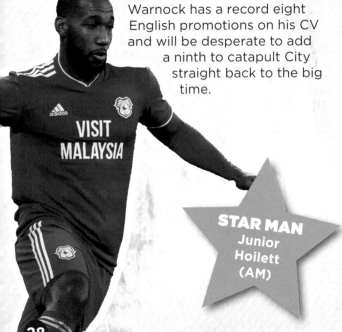

**STAR MAN**
Junior Hoilett (AM)

### FULHAM

| | |
|---|---|
| **MANAGER** | Scott Parker |
| **NICKNAME** | The Cottagers / Whites |
| **GROUND** | Craven Cottage |
| **CAPACITY** | 25,700 |
| **DISTANCE FROM W12** | 3.4 miles (17 mins) |
| **2018/19 POSITION** | 19th (Premier League) |

AFTER winning promotion to the Premier League via the play-offs in 2018 thanks to their impressive brand of free-flowing football under Slavisa Jokanovic, Fulham had a season to forget in the top-flight last time around.

The Cottagers spent big last summer, and it's safe to say that things didn't work out thereafter – Fulham comfortably relegated from the top tier in the end.

However, they do have some talented players in their squad and, if new boss Scott Parker can get the Whites motoring, a tilt for promotion this year wouldn't be a big surprise.

**STAR MAN**
Aleksandar Mitrovic (ST)

STAR MAN
Alex
Pritchard
(AM)

## ON THE UP

## FROM THE TOP

## HUDDERSFIELD TOWN

| MANAGER | Jan Siewert |
|---|---|
| NICKNAME | The Terriers |
| GROUND | John Smith's Stadium |
| CAPACITY | 24,500 |
| DISTANCE FROM W12 | 190.0 miles (3 hrs 32 mins) |
| 2018/19 POSITION | 20th (Premier League) |

## LUTON TOWN

| MANAGER | Graeme Jones |
|---|---|
| NICKNAME | The Hatters |
| GROUND | Kenilworth Road |
| CAPACITY | 10,356 |
| DISTANCE FROM W12 | 34.4 miles (52 mins) |
| 2018/19 POSITION | 1st (League One) |

RANGERS are set to renew acquaintances with Luton Town in the league for the first time since 2007.

AGAINST all odds, a fearless Huddersfield Town impressively staved off relegation from the Premier League in 2017/18 – but last season proved a bridge too far for the Terriers.

Town only gained a total of 16 points in total for 2018/19, finishing the campaign some 20 off 17th-placed Brighton. Popular former boss David Wagner was also replaced by fellow German Jan Siewert.

In truth, Siewert's task when appointed in January was an unenviable one – Huddersfield already 11 points from safety with just 15 Premier League games remaining. So he'll be hoping to guide the Terriers to better things with a full pre-season negotiated and campaign to look forward to.

The Hatters have since dipped into non-league – but are now firmly back on the rise and won the League One title thanks to a brand of passing football under Nathan Jones and then Mick Harford last term.

Town were last in the English top-flight in 1992 and will be hoping to use the momentum gained from promotion during their first season in the second tier for 12 years.

STAR MAN
James
Collins
(ST)

## BARNSLEY

| MANAGER | Daniel Stendel |
|---|---|
| NICKNAME | The Reds / Tykes |
| GROUND | Oakwell |
| CAPACITY | 23,287 |
| DISTANCE FROM W12 | 176.5 miles (3 hrs 12 mins) |
| 2018/19 POSITION | 2nd (League One) |

SECOND to Luton in League One, Barnsley also won automatic promotion to the Championship with a high-octane style of football.

Promotion was achieved in German boss Daniel Stendel's first season at the helm, and he'll be hoping his pressing approach will be as successful as it was for South Yorkshire neighbours Sheffield United on their return to this level. Chris Wilder's Blades won promotion from League One in 2016/17 before their rise to the Premier League last term.

Barnsley's main goal threat comes from forward Cauley Woodrow, who hit 19 goals in all competitions in 2018/19.

STAR MAN Mike-Steven Bahre (AM)

## CHARLTON ATHLETIC

| MANAGER | Lee Bowyer |
|---|---|
| NICKNAME | The Addicks |
| GROUND | The Valley |
| CAPACITY | 27,111 |
| DISTANCE FROM W12 | 15.2 miles (1 hr 8 mins) |
| 2018/19 POSITION | 3rd (League One, promoted via play-offs) |

CHARLTON had one of the strongest squads in League One last term but had to book their place in this year's Championship line-up via the play-offs, such was the competition for automatic promotion.

Lee Bowyer's side beat Sunderland in the showpiece Wembley final – and Rangers fans will welcome another London derby, as opposed to the long trip to the North East.

The Addicks were last a Premier League outfit 12 years ago and will have designs on pushing ever closer to a return this season.

## 2019/20 SKY BET CHAMPIONSHIP LINE-UP: IN FULL

Barnsley
Birmingham City
Blackburn Rovers
Brentford
Bristol City
Cardiff City
Charlton Athletic
Derby County

Fulham
Huddersfield Town
Hull City
Leeds United
Luton Town
Middlesbrough
Millwall
Nottingham Forest

Preston North End
Queens Park Rangers
Reading
Sheffield Wednesday
Stoke City
Swansea City
West Bromwich Albion
Wigan Athletic

# QUEENS PARK RANGERS
# SEASON 2019/20

# FREEMAN'S ON FIRE!

**MIDFIELD** playmaker Luke Freeman was named as QPR's Sportito Supporters' Player of the Year for the 2018/19 season.

The accolade was one of several gongs that Freeman won as part of the end-of-season vote, with the 27-year-old also being named as the Ray Jones Players' Player of the Year and the Junior Hoops Player of the Year.

Freeman provided six assists for his teammates last term, also bagging eight goals himself.

In the Players' Player vote, Freeman saw off competition from second-placed **Joe Lumley** and third-placed **Mass Luongo**. Lumley also finished second in the supporters' vote, with **Toni Leistner** coming third.

Elsewhere, youngster **Bright Osayi-Samuel** won the Daphne Biggs Supporters' Young Player of the Year award. Osayi-Samuel played 32 matches, scoring three goals.

And finally, Rs fan **Robert Hanafan** was named as the club's Supporter of the Year for '18/19.

# ROLL OF HONOUR

**Sportito Supporters' Player of the Year**
Luke Freeman

**Ray Jones Players' Player of the Year**
Luke Freeman

**Daphne Biggs Supporters' Young Player of the Year**
Bright Osayi-Samuel

**Junior Hoops Player of the Year**
Luke Freeman

**Supporter of the Year**
Robert Hanafan

# QUICK-FIRE QUIZ: 2018/19

**How well do you remember Rangers' previous Sky Bet Championship campaign? Here's 20 random but related questions for you…**

1. The R's kicked off their season with a slender defeat against which club?

2. Who was QPR's number 11 during the '18/19 campaign?

3. Who began the season as our first team manager?

4. Who did our first league win of the campaign come against, at the end of August?

5. This Brighton & Hove Albion loanee scored on his R's debut during that game in W12?

6. Who was named club captain ahead of the season, following his summer switch from Union Berlin?

7. Rangers reached the fifth round of the FA Cup, bowing out after a 1-0 defeat to eventual finalists Watford. Who did we beat to progress in the third round in January?

8. Which R's midfielder spent time on loan at Rotherham United?

9. Who was our top goalscorer in all competitions during the campaign?

10. Our biggest win of the season was 4-0, achieved against who at home in April?

11. It was an afternoon to forget in mid-August, with a 7-1 defeat coming at West Bromwich Albion. Who scored our consolation effort that day?

12. QPR picked up just a solitary red card in the league last term, against Stoke City in March. Which Rangers player was dismissed that day?

13. Who was sent off in our EFL Cup defeat at Blackpool in late September?

14. A season's double was achieved over two teams. Can you name them?

15. In which league position did the R's finish?

16. We used two goalkeepers throughout the campaign. Joe Lumley was one – can you name the other?

17. Our biggest home crowd was 17,609. Who was this against?

18. Who made the most QPR appearances over all competitions?

19. And what about the most substitute appearances?

20. On the final day, we rounded off our league season by winning 2-1 at Sheffield Wednesday. Where do the Owls play their home fixtures?

# SPOT THE DIFFERENCE

**Can you spot the 8 differences in the two images below?**

**ALL ANSWERS ON PAGE 61!**

**HE'S ONE OF OUR OWN**
# CLIVE ALLEN

# Loft legends who've come through the ranks in W12…

CLIVE Allen marked his first full start for QPR by scoring a magnificent treble in our 5-1 home win over Coventry City in April 1979.

"It was a brilliant time for me," said Allen, who still remembers the hat-trick with great fondness. "I grew up at Rangers. I first came along as a young kid to watch my dad Les play for, and then manage, the club.

"In fact, when I was six years old, I signed a piece of paper for R's chairman Jim Gregory. Then on the day when I was offered my first pro contract at the age of 17, Mr. Gregory pulled the original scrap of paper out of the top drawer of his desk and said, 'I told you that you were going to sign for QPR one day!'

"Overall, it was a great education for me as a person, and as a footballer. So I will always remember that and I will always have a soft spot for Queens Park Rangers."

"I grew up at Rangers. I first came along as a young kid to watch my dad Les play for, and then manage, the club"

Born in Stepney, east London on 20th May 1961, Allen came up through the youth ranks in W12. He played 157 matches in two spells for Rangers – hitting the net 83 times – and won the first three of his five England caps as an R's man.

Allen is best remembered at QPR for scoring the winning goals for us in the 1982 FA Cup quarter-final versus Crystal Palace, and the semi-final against West Brom.

Unfortunately, Clive limped off injured early in the final at Wembley when we faced Spurs, who he would later represent. But he'll always be remembered with great affection by Rangers fans.

# BEST AWAY WIN
# IT HAPPENED!

**AFTER 84 years of hurt, it finally happened! QPR won at the City Ground for the first time ever last December.**

Toni Leistner's header at the end of the first half proved to be the difference between the two sides in a 1-0 success, ending a run of 34 failed attempts at the home of Nottingham Forest.

In a game of few clear-cut chances, the game was decided by a powerful header from the R's centre-back just before the break.

In front of more than 1,500 delighted travelling R's fans, the wait was finally over.

# EBERE EZE

**Nationality:**
England

**Position:**
Attacking midfield

**Married:**
No

**Children:**
No

**Car:**
Audi Q8

**Favourite TV Programme:**
Game of Thrones

**Favourite Player:**
Ronaldinho

**Most Promising Teammate:**
Ilias Chair

**Favourite Other Team:**
Arsenal

**Childhood Footballing Hero:**
Ronaldinho

**Favourite Other Sport:**
Table tennis

**Most Difficult Opponent So Far:**
Marc Bola (Middlesbrough)

**Most Memorable Match:**
Millwall at home last season (scored in 2-0 win)

**Biggest Disappointment:**
Finishing 19th last year – that was too low.

**Favourite Meal:**
Lasagne and a Supermalt!

**Misc. Like:**
I once had a goldfish named Nemo!

**Favourite Holiday Destination:**
Bahamas

**Favourite Personality:**
Kevin Hart

**Favourite Activity On Day Off:**
Relaxing with mates

**Favourite Musician / Band:**
Tory Lanez

**Post-Match Routine:**
Go home, eat Mum's food, sleep!

**Best Friend:**
Two – Marc Bola and Dajon Golding

**Biggest Career Influence:**
Dad

**Personal Ambition:**
Play in the Champions League

**If You Weren't A Footballer, What Would You Be:**
It wasn't an option!

**Person In World You'd Most Like To Meet:**
Lionel Messi

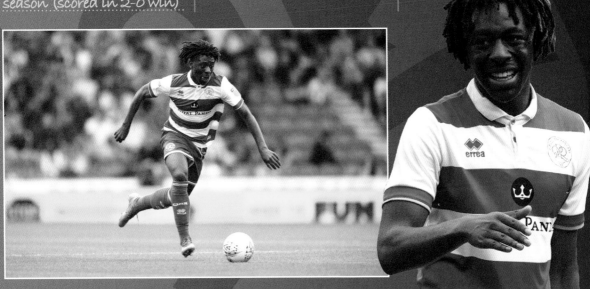

# HOW TO...
# HEADING

Heading is an integral part of both defending and attacking in football. QPR centre-half Grant Hall provides five essential pointers to consider when going up to win a headed challenge...

## 1. CONNECTION

Connection and timing are probably the most important aspects when it comes to heading the ball, because it's vital that you make a good connection with it. If you get the timing of your jump right, you've crossed the first big hurdle of making a successful connection with your header.

## 2. BALL FLIGHT

Where is the ball coming from? How much speed is on the ball? This then helps you to decide on what type of header you want to produce. Do you want to flick it on? Cushion it into someone's path? Head it clear or towards goal?

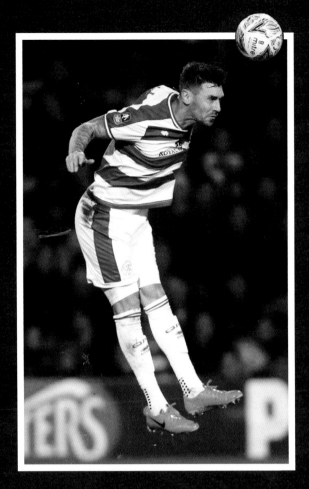

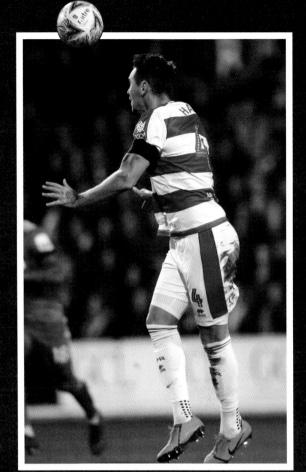

## 3. DISTANCE

If you are attempting to make a clearance, it's important that you fully commit to what you're doing. Keep your eyes on the ball and give it everything you've got if so.

## 4. ACCURACY

The higher the level you play at, the better teams and players are at finding teammates with headers. While it's not always possible to retain possession, keeping your composure when possible will help to do so.

## 5. AWARENESS

Being aware of what is around you is also important. Are you going to have to challenge an opponent when heading the ball? Do you need to get leverage, using your arms, giving a little bit of a nudge, to give yourself an advantage and win one?

**YOANN BARBET**

44

**DOMINIC BALL**

# GOAL OF THE SEASON
# LUKE LETS FLY!

**NOT content with sweeping up most of Rangers' end-of-season player awards, Luke Freeman's effort in QPR's entertaining New Year's Day draw at Aston Villa was voted Kiyan Prince Goal of the Year for 2018/19.**

Despite trailing to a 21st-minute Tammy Abraham strike, Freeman's firecracker four minutes before the break meant the R's went in at half-time level.

Rangers then took the lead in the 57th minute, with Ebere Eze finishing in devastating fashion following a free-flowing QPR move.

Honours would eventually end even however, with Abraham's second goal of the match in the 75th minute making it 2-2 – which is how this entertaining Sky Bet Championship affair finished.

# KEVIN
# GALLEN

# Loft legends who've come through the ranks in W12...

KEVIN Gallen fulfilled a boyhood dream when he scored 97 goals in 403 appearances for the R's – putting him seventh in our all-time list of QPR goalscorers.

Born on 21st September 1975 in West London, Gallen was a powerful striker and a lifelong Rangers supporter.

He had a prolific upbringing with the R's, his goalscoring achievements shattering Jimmy Greaves' all-time record at youth level. This led to England school, youth and Under-21 caps.

Gallen made his full debut away to Manchester United in a 2-0 defeat in August 1994 in the Premier League. The following midweek, his home debut was marked with a crisply-taken goal in the 3-2 victory against Sheffield Wednesday.

He had two spells at QPR and one of his best moments was scoring the opening goal in our famous 3-1 promotion-clinching win versus Sheffield Wednesday at Hillsborough in 2004.

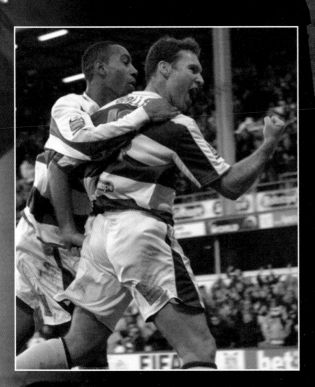

"My dad Jim began going to Rangers in the late 1960s and he still has a season ticket. He started to bring my two brothers, Joe and Steve, and me when we were old enough"

"Everyone in my family supports the R's," Gallen said. "My dad Jim began going to Rangers in the late 1960s and he still has a season ticket. He started to bring my two brothers, Joe and Steve, and me when we were old enough.

"I was the youngest so I began going to QPR around 1978/79. I can't really recall my first match, but I do remember games from the 1982 FA Cup run onwards.

"It was a dream come true to play for the Hoops. I adore the club – it is a lovely stadium at Loftus Road and the supporters are really fantastic."

# BEST DERBY WIN
# BEES STUNG!

## RANGERS' best London derby performance last season came in November.

A ten minute purple patch saw the R's score three goals, and come from behind to take victory in this rip-roaring West London battle at Loftus Road.

In some atrocious W12 rain, Championship hotshot Neal Maupay registered his 12th league goal of the campaign to hand Brentford a 22nd-minute lead.

QPR responded in empathic fashion to ultimately secure all three points and rise to 10th in the table.

Massimo Luongo (50) got the ball rolling for the R's, before further goals from Joel Lynch (58) and Nahki Wells (60) at the Loft End gave the Hoops a commanding lead.

The Bees did respond with a second goal through Henrik Dalsgaard in the 81st minute, though couldn't add a third during a tense finale.

51

GEOFF CAMERON

JOSH SCOWEN

# FOCUS ON
# OLAMIDE
# SHODIPO

**Nationality:**
Republic of Ireland

**Position:**
Winger

**Married:**
No

**Children:**
No

**Car:**
Range Rover Evoque

**Favourite TV Programme:**
Prison Break

**Favourite Player:**
Lionel Messi & Eden Hazard

**Most Promising Teammate:**
Eze, Chair & Osayi-Samuel

**Favourite Other Team:**
Arsenal

**Childhood Footballing Hero:**
Thierry Henry

**Favourite Other Sport:**
Table tennis

**Most Difficult Opponent So Far:**
Osman Kakay in training!

**Most Memorable Match:**
QPR debut v Leeds

**Biggest Disappointment:**
Injuries

**Favourite Meal:**
Chicken and rice

**Misc. Like:**
I like playing FIFA

**Favourite Holiday Destination:**
Jamaica

**Favourite Personality:**
Meek Mill

**Favourite Activity On Day Off:**
Meeting friends

**Favourite Musician / Band:**
Lil Baby, Meek Mill, A Boogie

**Post-Match Routine:**
Go home, chill & pray

**Best Friend:**
School mates Junior & Liban

**Biggest Career Influence:**
Dad

**Personal Ambition:**
Play at the highest possible level

**If You Weren't A Footballer, What Would You Be?**
I would have gone to uni, studying business management

**Person In World You'd Most Like To Meet:**
Lionel Messi

# HOW TO...

# DRIBBLING

Fans love players who can beat their marker – but how's best to do it? Hoops winger Bright Osayi-Samuel gives five hints on how to beat a full-back...

## 1. CONCENTRATION

Paint a picture before the ball has even arrived at your feet, always have a good look around you and stay concentrated.

## 2. CONFIDENCE

Probably one of the most important aspects of dribbling. If you want to beat your marker, have the confidence to beat them and go for it!

### 3. WHAT'S AROUND YOU?

Is there enough space for you to do what you want to do? Do you have the time to take your marker on? Would failing to complete a dribble put your team in trouble?

### 4. POSITION

Where you are on the pitch is very important. Ideally, you want to be in the final third of the pitch so that you can fully express yourself. Attempting to dribble near your own penalty area is obviously dangerous.

### 5. BE YOURSELF!

It's always good to do your research on the players you're about to come up against. However, don't let that put you off what you do best!

# WORDSEARCH

See if you can pick out these 10 R's stars...

| | | | | | | | | | | |
|---|---|---|---|---|---|---|---|---|---|---|
| T | Y | B | Q | B | L | M | H | A | L | L |
| C | Z | T | D | N | A | X | Z | N | O | L |
| L | N | N | P | N | T | K | Y | C | P | U |
| V | E | Y | N | V | D | K | S | L | I | M |
| L | L | I | N | N | E | V | O | T | D | L |
| R | N | K | S | Z | E | K | M | L | O | E |
| G | P | J | E | T | G | W | A | L | H | Y |
| B | B | B | R | Y | N | M | O | T | S | J |
| Z | C | F | N | G | Z | E | I | C | F | K |
| Y | F | Z | F | V | Z | M | R | M | S | Y |
| L | E | U | M | A | S | I | Y | A | S | O |

Amos

Eze

Hall

Leistner

Lumley

Manning

Osayi-Samuel

Scowen

Shodipo

Smith

**ALL ANSWERS ON PAGE 61!**

**ANGEL RANGEL**

# QUIZ ANSWERS

## P34: QUICK-FIRE QUIZ: 2018/19

1. Preston North End

2. Josh Scowen

3. Steve McClaren

4. Wigan Athletic

5. Tomer Hemed

6. Toni Leistner

7. Leeds United

8. Ryan Manning

9. Nahki Wells, 9

10. Swansea City

11. Joel Lynch

12. Grant Hall

13. Jordan Cousins

14. Ipswich Town & Sheffield Wednesday

15. 19th

16. Matt Ingram

17. Brentford

18. Luke Freeman, 48

19. Matt Smith, 31

20. Hillsborough

## P35: SPOT THE DIFFERENCE

## P59: WORDSEARCH

| T | Y | B | Q | B | L | M | H | A | L | L |
|---|---|---|---|---|---|---|---|---|---|---|
| C | Z | T | D | N | A | X | Z | N | O | L |
| L | N | N | P | N | T | K | Y | C | P | U |
| V | E | Y | N | V | D | K | S | L | I | M |
| L | L | I | N | N | E | V | O | T | D | L |
| R | N | K | S | Z | E | K | M | L | O | E |
| G | P | J | E | T | G | W | A | L | H | Y |
| B | B | B | R | Y | N | M | O | T | S | J |
| Z | C | F | N | G | Z | E | I | C | F | K |
| Y | F | Z | F | V | Z | M | R | M | S | Y |
| L | E | U | M | A | S | I | Y | A | S | O |

# QUEENS PARK RANGERS SKY BET CHAMPIONSHIP 2019/20 SEASON FIXTURES

| DATE | OPPONENTS | H / A | KICK-OFF |
|------|-----------|-------|----------|
| **AUGUST** | | | |
| SATURDAY 3 | STOKE CITY | A | 3PM |
| SATURDAY 10 | HUDDERSFIELD TOWN | H | 3PM |
| TUESDAY 13 | BRISTOL CITY (CARABAO CUP ROUND 1) | H | 7.45PM |
| SATURDAY 17 | BRISTOL CITY | A | 3PM |
| WEDNESDAY 21 | SWANSEA CITY | H | 7.45PM |
| SATURDAY 24 | WIGAN ATHLETIC | H | 3PM |
| WEDNESDAY 28 | PORTSMOUTH (CARABAO CUP ROUND 2) | H | 7.45PM |
| SATURDAY 31 | SHEFFIELD WEDNESDAY | A | 3PM |
| **SEPTEMBER** | | | |
| SATURDAY 14 | LUTON TOWN | H | 3PM |
| SATURDAY 21 | MILLWALL | A | 3PM |
| WEDNESDAY 25 | CARABAO CUP ROUND 3 | – | – |
| SATURDAY 28 | WEST BROMWICH ALBION | H | 12:30PM |
| **OCTOBER** | | | |
| WEDNESDAY 2 | CARDIFF CITY | A | 7.45PM |
| SATURDAY 5 | BLACKBURN ROVERS | H | 3PM |
| SATURDAY 19 | HULL CITY | A | 3PM |
| TUESDAY 22 | READING | H | 7.45PM |
| SATURDAY 26 | BRENTFORD | H | 3PM |
| WEDNESDAY 30 | CARABAO CUP ROUND 4 | – | – |
| **NOVEMBER** | | | |
| SATURDAY 2 | LEEDS UNITED | A | 3PM |
| SATURDAY 9 | MIDDLESBROUGH | H | 3PM |
| SATURDAY 23 | FULHAM | A | 3PM |
| WEDNESDAY 27 | NOTTINGHAM FOREST | H | 7.45PM |
| SATURDAY 30 | DERBY COUNTY | A | 3PM |
| **DECEMBER** | | | |
| SATURDAY 7 | PRESTON NORTH END | H | 3PM |
| WEDNESDAY 11 | BIRMINGHAM CITY | A | 7.45PM |
| SATURDAY 14 | BARNSLEY | A | 3PM |